D0838384

Rest
in
Peace.

IT'S TRUE!

HAUNTINGS HAPPEN
AND GHOSTS
GET GRUMPY

Other  titles

www.annickpress.com/microsites/itstrue.html

Meredith Costain

PICTURES BY Craig Smith

IT'S TRUE!

HAUNTINGS HAPPEN
AND GHOSTS
GET GRUMPY

annick press
toronto + new york + vancouver

Annick Press Ltd.
First published in Australia by Allen & Unwin.

Proofread by Helen Godolphin
Production of this edition by Antonia Banyard
Cover photographs: Getty Images/Ellen Schuster (headless man),
istockphoto.com/Steve Rabin (lightning) and Niels Laan (clouds moon)
Set in 12.5pt Minion by Ruth Grüner

Cataloging in Publication
Costain, Meredith
It's true! hauntings happen and ghosts get grumpy /
Meredith Costain ;
pictures by Craig Smith.

Includes index.
ISBN-13: 978-1-55451-022-1 (bound)
ISBN-10: 1-55451-022-8 (bound)
ISBN-13: 978-1-55451-021-4 (pbk.)
ISBN-10: 1-55451-021-X (pbk.)

1. Parapsychology. I. Smith, Craig, 1955– II. Title.
BF1461.C675 2006   133   C2006-901255-5

Printed in Canada

1 3 5 7 9 10 8 6 4 2

Published in the U.S.A. by
Annick Press (U.S.) Ltd.

Distributed in Canada by:
Firefly Books Ltd.
66 Leek Crescent
Richmond Hill, ON
L4B 1H1

Distributed in the U.S.A. by:
Firefly Books (U.S.) Inc.
P.O. Box 1338
Ellicott Station
Buffalo, NY 14205

Visit our website at: www.annickpress.com

CONTENTS

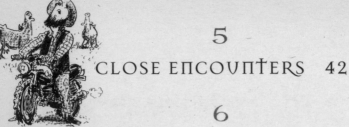

WHY THE SUPERNATURAL?

My grandmother was peeling potatoes at the sink when she had a sudden "vision." She saw her mother, 17,000 kilometers (10,600 miles) away in the north of England, waving goodbye to her. The next day Gran received a telegram that said her mother had died—at exactly the same time she'd "seen" her the day before.

My mother often has dreams about events that are about to take place and I seem to have a knack for prediction too. If I feel something really, really bad is going to happen, it usually does. (My computer crashed twice while I was typing that sentence.) And if I suddenly start thinking about my mum or sister, and check the clock, the display will usually read 11:11. I don't know if some kind of "sixth sense" runs in my family. What I do know is that I'm interested in things that science can't always explain.

Meredith Costain

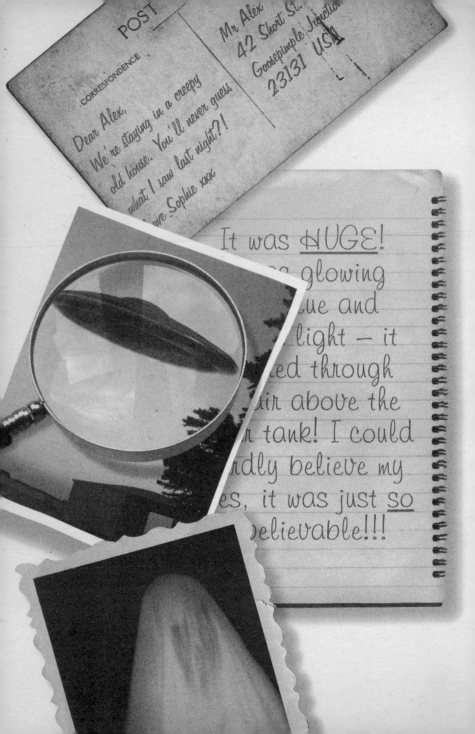

BELIEVE IT OR NOT . . .

Do you ever make predictions that seem to come true? Do you ever feel a spooky "presence" next to you when you think you're alone? Have you ever seen a UFO? "Skeptics" believe there are logical, scientific explanations for all these events. "Believers" think they are caused by supernatural, or spiritual, forces which are beyond our understanding.

This book is full of ghostly hauntings, mysterious disappearances, puzzling powers of the mind and contact with beings from out of this world. Are the stories true? Certainly they're very real to the people who recounted them. It's up to you to decide whether you're a skeptic or a believer—or maybe a little bit of both . . . .

I

THINGS THAT GO BUMP IN THE NIGHT

Enfield, England, August 1977

Peggy Harper rushed to her children's bedroom and switched on the light. Janet and Peter stopped screaming and stared at her, their eyes wide with terror.

"We heard a shuffling sound," Janet whispered. "Like a chair being dragged across the floor."

Peggy told her kids to stop goofing around and go to sleep. She turned off the light and left the room. As soon as she was outside the door she heard a shuffling noise, followed by four loud knocks.

Peggy raced back into the room. A heavy chest of drawers slid along the floor towards her. Peggy pushed it back into place, but as soon as she turned away the chest began moving again! She grabbed her four children from their bedrooms and herded her family across the garden to safety next door.

After this scare, Peggy contacted the Society for Psychical Research—experts in supernatural events. Over the next two years, the society documented over 1500 "strange happenings" at the Harper house. Furniture threw itself down stairs. Marbles flew across the room. Fires broke out in cupboard drawers. A plastic block soared through the air, hitting a newspaper photographer on the side of the head.

The trouble affected 11-year-old Janet the most. Night after night she was thrown from her bed and around the room. One morning she woke to find the curtains wrapped around her neck, as if someone was trying to strangle her. She began to speak in a deep male voice. The voice announced that it belonged to a man named Bill who had lived and died in the house years before.

THE FACE-SLAPPING GHOST

Adams Station, Tennessee, 1817

The Enfield haunting was blamed on a poltergeist, which is German for "noisy ghost." Poltergeists are famous for playing tricks on people by moving things around. In 1817, the Bell family of Tennessee had a brush with a scary poltergeist of their own.

According to a book written 25 years later by one of the children, the "Bell Witch" terrorized the Bell family for four years. Each night they'd wake to find their furniture upside-down or the sound of chained dogs fighting in their rooms. The family's nine children had their blankets yanked off, their hair pulled and their faces slapped while they slept. The ghost also made disgusting gulping, gurgling and choking noises.

The Bell Witch spent most of her time annoying 12-year-old Betsy. In fact, nothing much happened at the Bell house unless Betsy was in the room. Rumors buzzed around the neighborhood that she was putting it all on. When the ghost started to speak in a human voice, neighbors accused Betsy of "throwing" her own voice, in the same way ventriloquists make their dummies speak. A doctor tested this theory by covering Betsy's mouth with his hand while the ghost was speaking—but neither her lips nor her vocal cords moved once.

GHOULIES AND GHOSTIES

Have you ever seen a ghost? Was it legless or
headless?—or maybe only *partly* headless,
like Nearly Headless Nick, the Gryffindor ghost
from the Harry Potter books. Some ghosts are said
to appear as misty, shadowy forms. Others might
show up as balls of glowing energy or stinky fire.
Some ghosts are kind. Others are mean, cruel and
scary. But ghosts can't always be seen. Judging by
the most common reports of hauntings, you are
much more likely to hear, smell or feel the presence
of a ghost than actually see one.

THE HORROR IN THE CELLAR

Melbourne, Australia, 1978

Ten-year-old Laila Dickson was bored. Grabbing a flashlight, she and her friend Amanda Oleson climbed down to the cellar—a series of rooms underneath her 100-year-old house—to look for treasure. By the time they had squeezed their way along the narrow passages to the final room, they realized something was terribly wrong. Every hair on their arms was standing on end. The air in the room was bitterly cold—much colder than in the rooms they'd just passed through.

Nervously, Laila shone her flashlight around the gloom. Suddenly she froze. There on the floor in front of them was a pile of earth, the exact size of . . . a body. The girls ran screaming back through the cellar rooms to the tiny door beneath the main staircase. They never went down there again.

Laila had always known there was something strange about the house. Over the years that her family lived there, doors slammed whenever they went to bed, coffeepots flew across the kitchen and loud raps came from the boarded-up chimney. Laila would come downstairs in the morning to find the fruit from the fruit bowl creatively rearranged all over the kitchen table. Each night she sensed "something" creeping up to her bedside just as she was going to sleep. It filled her room with the overwhelming scent of talcum powder and the sound of swishing taffeta.

Laila's scientist father always refused to believe that his house was haunted. But he changed his mind when the family moved out and the fruit-arranging

and rapping sounds continued. The women who were renting the house were so terrified they brought in an exorcist. He said he'd found not one ghost but three— two noisy poltergeists and the ghost of a young woman who'd been murdered in the basement.

POLTERGEISTS OR HEATING PIPES?

Some people believe that ghosts are the spirits of dead people who can't let go of life. Maybe they died a tragic death before their time, or want to help their relatives or get revenge. Perhaps they're attracted to happy memories.

But some people don't believe in ghosts at all. They account for ghostly noises and scary stories in other ways.

Creaking, knocking, squeaking, groaning or rattling sounds are often blamed on pesky spirits, but they can also be caused naturally.

❁ Wood or metal in a house can expand and contract

as the air temperature rises and falls, and this often makes spooky creaking and groaning noises.

✿ Pipes in central heating systems can make knocking sounds as they heat up.

✿ Animals walking on the roof, like opossums, pigeons or squirrels, sound like a ghostly presence walking about.

✿ Rats and mice can live in the walls of houses and make strange scraping, chewing and squeaking sounds.

But what about doors that shut by themselves and spooky swinging chandeliers?

✿ If a house is built on clay, the ground underneath the house expands or shrinks as the clay fills up with moisture

or dries out. This can cause door and window frames to move out of alignment, so that they swing open or slam shut very easily.

✿ The layout of a house can sometimes act as a wind tunnel so that an open window can make a door slam at the other end of the house, even though you don't notice the breeze.

TONGUELESS MOUTHS AND FESTERING HANDS

The ghost of a page boy has been sitting on the front steps of Scotland's Castle Glamis[*] for hundreds of years, waiting for his family to remember to let him in. A woman without a tongue is said to roam the grounds, tearing at her mouth. People have reported the howling of men left to die in a secret room. William Shakespeare was so impressed with the castle's eerie atmosphere he used it as the setting for his murder-filled play, *Macbeth*.

[*] pronounced *Glarms*

11

Scottish ghost-hunter Elliot O'Donnell tells a very spooky story about Glamis. Apparently, an Englishman named Mr. Vance visited the castle in the 1930s, looking for fossils. The castle gardener asked Mr. Vance to look at something interesting he had dug up near the castle tower. It was a hand. Not an ordinary hand, but a large deformed one, with huge knuckles. Mr. Vance could barely bring himself to touch it, but the gardener insisted he take it back to his hotel room.

That night, as he walked past a mirror, Mr. Vance saw a grisly black shape materializing behind him. As he watched in horror, the shape transformed into the hand—now green and festering. A scream died in his throat. He was no longer standing in his hotel room. Instead, bare stone walls surrounded him.

A small bed stood in the corner of the chamber. Something was in the bed. Something . . . alive. Terrified, Mr. Vance found himself being drawn towards the bed. A knife appeared in his hand. Then he was plunging the knife into the thing that lay beneath the blankets, stabbing and stabbing, over and over.

Just when he thought his mind would explode, he found himself back in his hotel room. The stone walls, the bed, the knife had all gone. Only the hand remained. The next morning he went back to the castle, desperate to give back the horrible hand. But no one had ever heard of the gardener. Mr. Vance himself returned the hand to its keeping place—the soil beneath the haunted tower of Castle Glamis.

FACES ON THE FLOOR

Bélmez, Spain, 1971
A creaky castle with towers and turrets seems like a natural home for a ghost. But sometimes they pop up in unexpected places.

On August 23, 1971, Maria Gomez Pereira was cooking breakfast in her kitchen. Without warning, a face appeared on the floor at her feet, its eyes wide with terror and pain. Over the next few days, the features grew stronger. Maria repeatedly scrubbed the floor but couldn't remove the face. She asked her son, Miguel, to smash the concrete floor with a sledgehammer and put in a new one.

Six days later, a different face appeared, in the same spot. This time the Pereira family dug underneath the house. Three meters (9.8 feet) down they found a pile of human bones—the remains of bodies buried in a cemetery hundreds of years before.

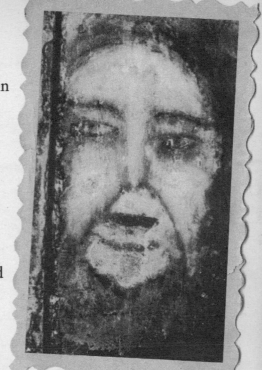

In the following years, many different faces appeared. Investigators came to the house, but no one found any evidence of paints or dyes that would have proved the faces were fakes. Tape recordings made while the house was empty contained baffling sounds when played back, including mysterious wails, whispers and cries. If you ever find yourself on a bus tour in southern Spain, ask the driver to stop at the village of Bélmez de la Moraleda, so you can see "The House of the Faces" for yourself!

Feel like doing a spot of ghostbusting yourself?

HERE'S WHAT YOU'LL NEED:

☆ **soft-soled shoes** So ghosts can't hear you coming.

☆ **a notebook and pen** To record sightings.

☆ **a flashlight** People say ghosts often won't make an appearance till the lights are turned out.

☆ **sticky notes** To mark exactly where the ghost materialized.

☆ **a camera with a flash and high-speed film** For taking photographs in low light.

☆ **a video camera with infrared film** For shooting footage in the dark.

☆ **a tape recorder** For capturing unearthly cries and wails.

☆ **spare batteries for all your electrical gear** Ghosts, especially poltergeists, love sabotaging equipment.

☆ **a thermometer** To measure falls in temperature.

☆ **a first-aid kit** In case of nasty run-ins with rough poltergeists—it's always better to be safe than sorry!

2

YOU CAN'T KEEP A GOOD GHOST DOWN

The taxi driver couldn't believe his eyes. He'd stopped to pick up a young blonde woman walking along the road that ran past the local cemetery. It was a cold night, and she was wearing a flimsy white dress. He turned round to talk to her, only to find the back seat was empty. The woman was gone.

RESURRECTION MARY

Some cities have famous ghosts who reportedly appear
again and again to different people, often years apart.
The people of Chicago, Illinois, are particularly proud
of their "own" special ghost, "Resurrection Mary."
Reports of a disappearing blonde began in the 1930s.
People driving down Archer Avenue claimed they'd
seen a young fair-haired woman in a white dress
trying to jump onto the running boards of their cars.

Some would offer her a ride, only to find that she'd mysteriously "vanish" from the car as they drove past Resurrection Cemetery. Other people claimed to have met the young woman in the O. Henry Ballroom. They'd dance with her, then offer her a lift home at the end of the night. As their car passed the cemetery, she would always disappear.

Some reports are far more gruesome. Several drivers saw the young woman rush out of the cemetery gates and stop right in front of their car. They described hearing the sickening thump as the front of the car plowed into her. But each time, weirdly, it was as if their car had gone right "through" her. The next thing they saw was her slim body disappearing through the gates of Resurrection Cemetery.

Reports of Mary have continued through the years. On August 10, 1976, a passerby saw a woman in a white dress locked inside the cemetery fence. It was late at night, so he called the police. But by the time the police arrived, the graveyard was deserted and two bars of the main gate—heavy bars, made of iron—had been bent outwards. The bars bore the clear prints of human hands. Cemetery officials tried to burn off the prints with a blowtorch. But you can still see them today, right there on the main gates.

So who was this strange woman in the white party dress? People have been trying to track down the "real" Mary for decades, but still nobody knows for sure. She might have been a girl killed while hitchhiking home after storming out of the O. Henry Ballroom. She might have been a young Polish woman who sneakily borrowed her father's car to visit her boyfriend and was killed in an accident. Whoever she was, she is now famous all over Chicago, and people driving down Archer Avenue still report seeing her trying to hitch a ride.

THEATER GHOSTS

Melbourne, Australia, 1888

The trapdoor opened. The audience watched spellbound as Federici, the opera singer playing the devil, sank dramatically down to the "fires of hell" below. At the end of the play the delighted crowd jumped to their feet, clapping furiously as the singer took his final bows alongside the rest of the cast.

But the real Federici was no longer on stage. As he was being lowered through the trapdoor to the area beneath, he'd had a massive heart attack. The audience had been clapping his ghost.

Over the years, many people have claimed to have seen the ghost of Federici (whose real name was Frederick Baker). The singer who took over Federici's role in the opera said he felt invisible hands push him backwards every time he took his bow at the end of the show. Stagehands and theater managers have felt him brush past them in the corridors and have seen him sitting in the dress circle, wearing a long cloak and a top hat. If he's spotted on the opening night of a show, it's seen as good luck! The Princess Theatre used to leave a seat empty in the second row especially for Federici's ghost.

A HAUNTING EXPERIENCE

Next time you visit one of these theaters,
keep an eye out for its resident ghost.

The Palace, Times Square, New York, NY

Over one hundred ghosts are said to haunt the Palace, including a cellist in a white dress playing in the orchestra pit, a sad little girl looking down from the balcony and the famous singer Judy Garland. But be warned—legend has it that anyone who sees the ghost of a tightrope walker who fell and broke his neck will soon die themselves!

Palace Grand Theatre, Dawson City, Yukon

The all-singing, all-dancing ghost of "Klondike Kate," a popular music hall entertainer who died in 1957, still haunts the upstairs dressing rooms today.

Avon Theater, Decatur, Illinois

Staff report hearing laughter, applause and footsteps coming from the theater long after it has emptied for the night. Some workers feel they are being watched or even touched by ghostly hands. Late-night sightings of a middle-aged man with short hair are thought to resemble a former owner.

The Music Box Theater, Chicago, Illinois

"Whitey"—a former manager of the theater—still likes to keep an eye on things. You can see him pacing near the door where kids like to sneak in.

Radio City Music Hall, New York, NY

The ghost of the Music Hall's builder, S.L. "Roxy" Rothafel, likes to appear on opening nights, on the arm of a glamorous woman.

THE PHANTOM FUNERAL GUEST

Eighty-four years after Federici was buried in the Melbourne General Cemetery, a film crew visited his grave. They were making a documentary about his life, called *The Devil in Evening Dress*. While they were filming a re-enactment of the burial service, a member of the cast took photos. One of the photos appears to show a shadowy phantom, wearing a long cloak, leaning against a tombstone. Federici watching his own funeral, perhaps?

3

IS ANYBODY OUT THERE?

On a cloudless night, lie on your back outside and look up at the sky. (If you can get out of the city and away from its distracting bright lights, all the better.) Big, isn't it!

The universe is huge—and growing larger all the time. If you hold up a nickel to the sky, you cover up more than 1000 different galaxies. That's a lot of stars and planets. Imagine how many there must be in the rest of the sky that you *haven't* covered! There's a whole cosmos out there for strange things to inhabit.

American astronomer Frank Drake calculated that there may be as many as 10 million stars just like our sun in the universe. If our small solar system contains a planet with living creatures on it, maybe one of the other 10 million does too. While we're wondering if there is "anybody out there," maybe a being is sitting on another planet, wondering the same thing. Spooky.

Our technology is not yet advanced enough for us to travel the universe, but some people believe that aliens have visited Earth. The American Air Force invented the term Unidentified Flying Object, or UFO, to refer to any object in the sky they didn't recognize.

When most people hear "UFO" they think of an alien spaceship hovering in our skies.

THEY CAME FROM THE SKY . . .

UFO sightings aren't new. People have been reporting strange things in the skies for centuries. In 1492, a sailor on Christopher Columbus's ship, the *Santa Maria*, reported seeing a "glittering thing" in the distance that would vanish and reappear. American Air Force pilots in World War II told their friends about glowing balls of fire in the sky that were definitely not lights from planes. They called them "foo fighters" after a term used in a comic strip that was popular at the time.

Some people believe UFO sightings are even older. A carving on the wall of the Egyptian temple of Abydos appears to be a flying saucer. A tombstone found in the ancient temple of Palenque in Mexico bears a carving that looks like an astronaut in a jet-propelled spaceship.

There may even be a UFO sighting in the Bible! In the first chapter of the Book of Ezekiel, Ezekiel sees a bronze-colored object appear from a glowing sky. It is made up of four creatures, each with four faces and four wings. Beside the creatures are giant wheels within wheels that make a thunderous noise. A vision from God—or an alien spacecraft?

THE FiRST FLYiNG SAUCERS

Cascade Mountains, Washington, 1947

The term "flying saucer" was first used by an American reporter from the *East Oregonian* newspaper in 1947. He interviewed a pilot, Kenneth Arnold, who had been searching for the wreckage of a military plane in the Cascade Mountains in Washington State. Nine bright objects had suddenly zoomed past Kenneth at incredible speed. He said the strange craft had boomerang-shaped wings and no tail. Kenneth also told the reporter they had whizzed across the sky like a hand-thrown saucer skipping across water. So the reporter used the term "flying saucers" when he wrote the story. The name stuck, even though the objects Kenneth had described were shaped more like crescents than saucers.

Kenneth Arnold's sighting sparked a flood of reports. Over the next two months, 850 people from all over the country claimed they'd seen UFOs, all shaped like flying saucers.

IDENTIFIED FLYING OBJECTS

Most UFOlogists (people who study UFOs) would agree that 95 percent of UFO sightings turn out to be natural or man-made objects. Once UFOs have been investigated and identified, they are called IFOs—Identified Flying Objects.

The things most commonly mistaken for UFOs are:

...Ha ha...
...buzz click...
this will fool
the earth!

- 🏵 the planet Venus
- 🏵 stars
- 🏵 aircraft lights
- 🏵 weather balloons
- 🏵 kites
- 🏵 satellites
- 🏵 shooting stars
- 🏵 the moon
- 🏵 saucer-shaped clouds lit by rays from a setting sun
- 🏵 strange electrical effects, such as ball lightning or

St. Elmo's Fire (St. Elmo's Fire is a halo of light that appears around pointy objects such as ships' masts or church steeples in bad weather.)

Other strange (but true) IFOs include:

- an owl that had eaten some glow-in-the-dark fungi
- city lights reflecting from the white stomachs of a flock of geese
- a swarm of insects affected by St. Elmo's Fire

How to record your own UFO sighting

If you've seen a UFO there are several sites on the Internet where you can report your experience. You could start with:

The National UFO Reporting Center
Go to www.nuforc.org

Sci Fi
Go to www.SCIFI.com
or send an e-mail to UFO@www.SCIFI.com

Experienced UFOlogists will review selected encounters and publish their findings at a UFOlogy center.

4

THE ROSWELL INCIDENT

The Foster Ranch, Roswell, New Mexico, 1947

Sheep rancher Mac Brazel was standing on his front porch when he was startled by a loud explosion. There were storms in the area that night, so he figured it was probably just thunder. The next morning he rode out to check his livestock. Something shiny caught his eye. Down in the valley below was what looked like the remains of a wrecked plane.

A few days later, Brazel drove into town for a drink at his local pub. Everyone was talking about the strange UFO they'd seen whizzing across the night sky. That got Brazel thinking. Maybe the shiny thing in his paddock was a UFO too! He rang the sheriff to tell him his theory.

WEIRD WRECKAGE

The sheriff got in touch with the local airbase at Roswell. The Air Force sent an intelligence officer, Major Jesse Marcel, to Brazel's farm to check out the wreckage. Major Marcel thought the stuff on the ground was so weird he took some of it home to show his wife and kids. Part of the wreckage seemed to be some kind of light metal. It looked a bit like foil, but when Major Marcel bashed it with a sledgehammer, the metal didn't even dent. The Marcels couldn't cut it, burn it or bend it.

WEIRDER AND WEIRDER

Meanwhile, 300 kilometers (186 miles) away, something even weirder was going on. Grady Barnett, out working in the desert, came across a disc-shaped aircraft that had crashed into a hillside. Lying next to the craft were four of the strangest "bodies" he'd ever seen. Dressed in tight gray one-piece suits, the bodies were thin, with frail limbs. They had big hairless heads, with large eyes and only a slit for a mouth.

A jeep full of soldiers zoomed up. They sealed off the area and gave Barnett strict instructions to get out of there—fast. They also told him not to tell anyone else about what he'd seen that day. Then they began packing up the remains of the crashed craft. Later that night, heavily guarded transporter planes took off from Roswell Airbase, bound for a base in Ohio.

THE ARMY CHANGES ITS MIND

The next day Lieutenant Walter Haut, an information officer from Roswell Airbase, gave local newspapers a huge scoop. A flying saucer had crash-landed in the area! UFO fever swept across the country—until Lieutenant Haut pulled the rug out from under his own story a few hours later. He announced that the "experts" who'd examined the craft had all made an "embarrassing" mistake. It hadn't been an alien spaceship at all. No siree. The wreckage that covered Brazel's valley was actually from a plain old weather balloon. The lieutenant even handed around pieces of the balloon at the press conference so journalists could examine them for themselves.

Meanwhile, back at the sheep ranch, Mac Brazel had been "safely removed" from the prying eyes and ears of reporters. When the Air Force finally let him go, Brazel had somehow lost the urge to talk about what he'd seen—even to his own family.

GRAVITY-BUSTERS

Most people who claim to have seen aliens say they are "humanoid" in shape. They describe beings that stand upright with two legs, two arms and a head with eyes, a nose and a mouth. But scientists don't think it's very likely that aliens would look like us. The human body has developed in the conditions and environment on Earth. If we lived on a planet that was twice the size of ours, the increase in gravity would mean our bones would be much heavier and we'd have to walk around on our hands and knees. So unless the aliens come from a planet exactly the same as ours, we can't really expect them to look much like us.

ALIEN AUTOPSY?

Over the next 50 years, conspiracy theories raged around the country. What really went on at Roswell? Why had the Air Force changed its story? Why had a lot of important files and eyewitnesses gone missing? Over 200 people came forward to say they'd seen the four bodies that had been taken from the crashed spacecraft. A nurse even claimed she'd seen doctors performing an autopsy on a body at the Air Force hospital!

In 1984, some UFOlogists produced a movie they'd been secretly sent which they claimed showed the autopsy taking place. In the film what looks like a small alien is lying on an operating table. It has no hair, large eyes, and only a slit for a mouth. It looks *exactly* like the bodies that Grady Barnett had described seeing lying near the wreckage of the disc-shaped aircraft all those years before.

WHAT _REALLY_ HAPPENED AT ROSWELL?

Fifty years after the crash, the Air Force finally came clean. The wreckage they'd shown reporters hadn't been from a weather balloon at all. It had come from a "Project Mogul" balloon. These balloons carried metal "listening" discs the Americans were using to spy on the Soviet Union's nuclear-testing program. Many people now believe that the wreckage Brazel and Barnett found that day was actually part of a top-secret device being tested by the US government.

After analyzing the events that happened in the Roswell area in 1947, investigators came up with the following explanations:

❃ Scientists at the White Sands missile range, near Roswell, were testing military equipment at the time of the crash. The wreckage could have been some kind of top-secret device being tested for the government.

❃ The extra-strong shiny material Major Marcel took home to show his family was probably an early form of polyethylene. Polyethylene is light and so strong it probably wouldn't dent if you banged it with a sledgehammer. It was invented around the time of the crash.

✿ In 1947, combat units based at Roswell Airbase were being trained to handle and drop nuclear bombs. Perhaps the heavily guarded transport planes that took off from the base that night were carrying nuclear weapons rather than bits of flying saucer.

✿ During the 1940s, the United States Air Force had been running experiments in the Roswell area, throwing crash-test dummies down to the ground from great heights. Crash-test dummies are dressed in tight-fitting one-piece suits, and have bald heads with minimal features . . . .

BUT WHAT ABOUT THE ALIEN AUTOPSY FILM?

A special-effects firm—expert in fooling people—has drawn up a long list of reasons why they think the film is a fake. You can check out their website at www.trudang.com/autopsy/autogoof.html

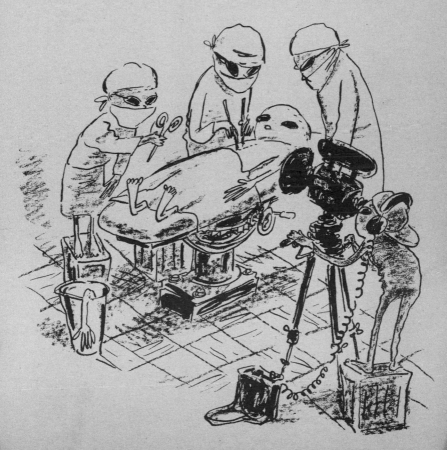

5

CLOSE ENCOUNTERS

UFOlogists classify contact with aliens into four levels of "close encounter."

1 The *first kind* is unexplained lights or objects in the sky.

2 The *second kind* is physical evidence, like parts of a spaceship or a burnt landing site.

3 The *third kind* is actually seeing, or being in contact with, aliens in or near a UFO.

4 The *fourth kind* is being abducted by aliens.

Most of the reported encounters with extraterrestrials are of the first kind. But sometimes people have even weirder stories to tell.

RUNNING AROUND IN CIRCLES

Duhamel, Alberta, 1967

In August 1967 six circular
impressions appeared in
a pasture near Duhamel,
Alberta. Weeks earlier, two
local girls had reported seeing
a large cream-colored disc

ahead of them, moving up and down through the air.

A military researcher, Mr. G. Jones, and two other
men went out to investigate the pasture. The grass looked
like it had been flattened by a heavy wheel moving in
a near-perfect circle. These marks, reported Jones,
were "quite distinct from car and truck tire marks."

But what kind of machine could have made the
circles? There were no footprints to suggest that
pranksters had been at work. The field was mowed
before the mystery had been solved.

Thirteen years later in England, a series of
mysterious patterns began appearing in farmers'
fields. The vegetation was flattened in spirals, discs, or

complicated shapes. These "crop circles" were huge—bigger than an average house. They began to appear in other countries, too.

Experts speculated about what made them—were they the work of aliens? Some said they were formed by mini-tornados. Another theory was that mating hedgehogs running around in frenzied circles made these strange shapes. Finally two Englishmen admitted that they were responsible. They even demonstrated how they'd used two pieces of wood and string to fake these alien landing sites.

But the incident in Alberta remains unexplained.

CUT-UP COWS

Over the years, there have been many reports from ranchers of livestock mutilation. Cows had their vital organs "surgically" removed without any loss of blood. Texan rancher Judy Doraty claims that aliens abducted her and forced her to watch while her cows were operated on.

ABDUCTIONS IN ARIZONA

Apache Sitgreaves National Forest, Arizona, 1975

Travis Walton and his crew of forestry workers were traveling home in their truck when the driver slammed on the brakes. Hovering above them was a large, glowing disc-shaped object. Travis got down from the truck to check it out, then suddenly changed his mind. Too late. A beam of light engulfed him.

Six days later, Travis's sister received a phone call. Her brother was in a phone booth outside their town. Safe at home, Travis told his family his frightening story. He said he'd woken from a deep sleep to find himself lying on an operating table in a brightly lit room. Three creatures were leaning over him— creatures with huge bald heads, large eyes and slitty mouths. He swung a piece of equipment at them, then bolted from the room.

Finding a window, he stared at the stars and galaxies of the universe spread out before him. He was zooming through space! After a while something tapped him on the shoulder. A humanoid led him out of the UFO and into a huge building. More disc-shaped craft were parked in the corner. A mask was placed over his face, and he was told to lie down. The next thing he knew, he was back on the highway outside his hometown. He'd "lost" five days of his life.

Sound too far-fetched to believe? Maybe it is. Skeptical investigators discovered some interesting facts about the case. Travis had recently seen a TV show about an American couple who claimed they'd been abducted. He'd talked about it a lot with his family. He was also accused of holding his breath to trick a lie-detector test, which he failed anyway. But wait, there's more. His story just happened to win the $5000 prize offered by a trashy national newspaper for reports of UFO sightings.

How to tell if you've experienced a close encounter of the fourth kind

Place a tick next to the events from the list below that have happened to you.

1. I have woken up paralyzed with a sense of a strange person or presence in the room. ☐

2. I have felt as if I were flying through the air, even though I didn't know how or why. ☐

3. I have had vivid dreams about UFOs. ☐

4. I have felt as if I have "left" my body and floated above it. ☐

5. I have seen frightening beings under my bed or in my wardrobe. ☐

6. I have puzzling scars on my body and I have no idea how they got there. ☐

7. I have seen unusual lights or balls of light in my room. ☐

8. I have "lost" at least an hour of time, without knowing where I was during that time. ☐

ALIEN IDENTIFICATION KIT

Grays

Description: Around 1.3 meters (4.3 feet) tall. Large head with huge dark eyes, tiny nose and mouth, and a pointy chin. Small, weak, gray or white body with translucent skin.

Activities: Appear in 70 percent of all reported human abductions. Perform medical tests on humans in a cold, clinical manner.

Habitat: All over the world. UFO generally parked nearby.

Humanoids

Description: Very similar to human beings—in fact, if you passed one in the street, you'd have trouble recognizing it as an alien.

Activities: In charge of human abductions. Communicate by telepathy.

Habitat: Most parts of the world.

Nordics

Description: Human-like shape, with long blonde hair and blue eyes.

Activities: Pilot well-built, safety-conscious UFOs and shop at Ikea.

Habitat: Europe and the United States.

Shadowy Projections

Description: Unformed and shadowy, often seen within glowing masses. Frequently accompanied by a buzzing or whistling sound.

Activities: Enjoy terrifying trained military personnel and guard dogs.

Habitat: Roads and highways. Usually accompanied by a UFO that resembles a large orange or green light.

DO YOU BELİEVE İN ALİEПS?

You might be surprised to find out how many people think we're not alone in the universe. In 2002, a market research company conducted a survey to discover what American people thought about aliens. Two-thirds believed that there were definitely other forms of intelligent life in the universe. Nearly half believed that UFOs have either visited the Earth in some form over the years, or that they are watching or listening in to what we are doing. More than one in three believe that humans have met up with extraterrestrial life forms, and one in five that humans have actually been abducted by aliens!

God help us – aliens are chasing us!

6

HERE ONE MINUTE, GONE THE NEXT...

Gloucester, England, 1906

The Vaughan children loved playing hide-and-seek in the trees, hedges and ditches of Forty Acre Field near their home. One strange day they didn't come home for tea so their parents went to look for them. After a long search, the Vaughans called the police.

For the next three days, a large search party combed the field, especially the hedges and the deep ditch that separated Forty Acre Field from a cornfield. Nothing was found. But, at six o'clock the following morning, a farm laborer on his way to work discovered the three

children lying asleep
—in the very same
ditch that had been
so carefully
searched the day
before. None of
the children had
any idea what
had happened
—all they
remembered
was going
to sleep.
Somehow, it
seems they'd
lost not only
themselves,
but three
days of
their lives . . . .

BEAM ME UP, SCOTTY

So what happened to the Vaughan children? Well, the mystery remains unsolved. Some people think they were kidnapped by a neighbor and hypnotized so they would forget their ordeal. Others think they disappeared right out of this world—teleported to another dimension.

Maybe it was just like the "Beam me up, Scotty!" scenes in *Star Trek*. When Captain Kirk and his crew stand on their transporting platform they dissolve into glitter. Next thing you know, they've re-materialized on another planet, or back on the *Enterprise*.

ZAPPING THROUGH TIME AND SPACE

Teleportation *is* scientifically possible—if you don't mind making a bit of a mess. First, you have to break down the atoms of a person or object in one place. Next, you send the details of how these atoms are put together to another place. Once the details arrive there, the atoms could be put together in exactly the same order.

Want to go to Disneyland but haven't got time because your mum's calling you to dinner? If you could use teleportation to get there, you wouldn't need to worry about how far away a place was, or how long it'd take to get there.

Sadly, teleportation is nowhere near that advanced yet. Australian scientists have made a beam of light disappear in one place and reappear a meter (3.3 feet) away. However, the original beam of light was destroyed in the process. The second beam of light was only a *copy* of the first one, not the real thing.

This doesn't make human teleportation look too promising. First of all, scientists would have to be able to pinpoint and analyze the different atoms that make up the human body—all trillion trillion of them. Next, the "tele-traveler" would have to be prepared to, well, die.

cool – it almost worked

Their original mind and body would no longer exist. Sure, their atomic structure would be put back together in the new location. The new "person" would be digitally programmed with the tele-traveler's memories, emotions, hopes and dreams but would only be a copy, not the real thing.

THE FOOT WITHOUT A BODY

St. Petersburg, Florida, 1951
Mary Reeser's landlady was getting worried. She hadn't seen the elderly widow for a while. She tried to enter Mary's apartment, then jumped back in shock.
The door handle was burning hot. The landlady's screams were so loud that two painters working up the street came running. Forcing open the door, they reeled back in horror at the gruesome scene before them.
On the floor lay a pool of grease, a pile of ash, a shrunken skull and a foot, still in its slipper.

Thirty-five years later, another body was found in spookily similar circumstances. New Yorker Kendall Mott found the remains of his father George—a piece of skull, part of a foot and a pile of ashes—in his bed one morning. Some of the furniture in his dad's room had been burnt. There had definitely been a fire of some kind. But how had it started? And why were some body parts left whole at the end?

One theory is that the bodies spontaneously combusted—that is, they suddenly burst into flames for no earthly reason. In the movie *Spinal Tap*, this happens to the heavy metal band's drummers all the time. One minute they're playing a furious drum solo, the next—pop!—they're consumed by flames.

Skeptic researchers Joe Nickell and John Fischer spent two years investigating the Mary Reeser case. They suggested that the destructive fire had a natural cause. Mary was a smoker and had taken several sleeping pills on the day of her death. Nickell and Fischer concluded that she had probably fallen asleep while still holding a burning cigarette. Then, in the same way a candle burns wax, the flame may have set her clothes alight then *very* slowly burnt her body fat. The bits of Mary and George that were left probably didn't contain enough fat to burn completely.

Or maybe they were sticking out, away from the hottest parts of the fire.

TRIANGLE OF DEATH

One place is more famous for disappearances than any other on Earth. I bet you've heard of the Bermuda Triangle. Over the last century there have been over 100 recorded

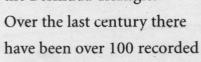

Are we there yet?

instances of ships or aircraft—carrying over 1000 people—disappearing in the triangle that lies between Bermuda, Puerto Rico and the southern tip of Florida.

What's causing all these ships and planes to disappear? One theory is that there is a magnetic "whirlpool" in the area that interferes with navigational equipment. But this doesn't explain the fact that ships and planes are often never seen again. Another theory is that the missing craft have entered a gateway to another world—the fourth dimension perhaps?

Tales from the Triangle

1492 While sailing through the Triangle, Christopher Columbus sees a large ball of fire fall into the sea. A later entry in his log records an account of a light that appeared over the water briefly before vanishing.

1918 The huge Navy vessel, USS *Cyclops*, disappears between Barbados and Baltimore. (Not sure if this is related to the disappearance, but apparently the eccentric captain liked to wear nothing but long underwear and a bowler hat while commanding his ship.)

1941 Two of the *Cyclops'* sister ships, the *Proteus* and the *Nereus*, disappear.

1945 Five US Airforce bombers disappear over the Triangle and are never seen again, and a sixth plane sent to look for them crashes into the sea. (On the day the planes took off, one lucky crew member had a premonition that something would go wrong and stayed behind.)

1969 Crew members from National Airlines flight 727 traveling across the Triangle are mystified to find on landing that all the plane's timepieces are 10 minutes slow. Their plane had disappeared from nearby radar screens for . . . exactly 10 minutes.

Skeptics believe that most of the stories about missing ships have been grossly exaggerated. They say the area—which is around a million square kilometers (621,000 square miles)—is no more dangerous than any other part of our oceans. They suggest other reasons for the loss of ships: tangling seaweed, circling currents, dangerous reefs, storms and water spouts. They also suggest that swift-flowing currents and deep trenches in the seabed make it hard to trace the wreckage of lost planes and ships.

7

PSYCHIC POWERS

Have you ever been thinking about a friend, then
moments later had a phone call from that person?
Or had a vivid dream or vision about an event that
comes true the following day? Did you ever think that
maybe you're psychic? Psychics possess extrasensory
perception (ESP), which is the ability to predict events
or control people with the power of the mind.

IT'S A LOTTERY

There are many stories of people making
huge sums of money by betting on horses
whose names came to them in dreams.
Other people have won the lottery by

using a sequence of numbers they dreamed about. Sometimes people's premonitions don't have such a happy result.

COAL MINE DISASTER

Aberfan, South Wales, 1966
Morning assembly at Pantglas Junior School had just finished. Kids and teachers headed off to their classrooms to start the day.

Meanwhile, Monica McBean was recovering in the washroom at the aircraft factory where she worked, over 300 kilometers (186 miles) away. She'd just had a disturbing "vision" that had seemed so real it gave her the creeps. She'd seen a "black mountain" come crashing down, burying a group of children.

As the schoolchildren reached their classrooms, half a million tons of coal waste came sliding down the mountain, engulfing the school. Parents and miners dug frantically, trying to locate survivors. Twenty-eight adults and 116 children were killed.

The day before the disaster, nine-year-old Eryl Mai Jones had been talking casually to her parents about death and dying. She'd told them she wasn't afraid to die because she knew that she'd be going to heaven with two of her best friends. Then she told them about a strange dream she'd had the night before. In the dream, she'd gone to school as usual but it hadn't been there. "Something black" had come down all over it. Eryl's body was pulled from the rubble of the school. On either side of her were her two best friends.

Are you psychic?

ZENER CARDS ARE USED TO TEST PEOPLE FOR ESP.
MAKE FIVE CARDS FOR EACH OF THE FIVE SYMBOLS.

Ask a friend to sit behind a screen or on the other side of the room so you can't see what they're doing. They should shuffle the cards, then turn them over one by one. As they turn up each card, they should use the power of their mind to telepathically "send" the image to your mind. See how often you can guess which card your friend has turned over.

Under the laws of probability, you have a one in five chance of guessing the correct answer each time. So if you keep getting a score that's much more than 5 out of 25, woo hoo! You're probably psychic.

PSYCHIC DETECTIVES

Psychic detectives believe they can use their powers of ESP to help police solve crimes.

In 2001, a California man brutally murdered his wife and 13-year-old daughter, then dismembered their bodies. But the body parts went missing from the place he'd dumped them. Enter Carla Baron, an experienced psychic with plenty of solved cases under her belt. One of her methods is to lay out tarot (fortune-telling) cards while she's looking at photos of a missing person.

Carla told investigators that she could "see" images of tall pillars, smoke and smokestacks. She concluded that the victims' bodies had been burned. Another strong feeling told her that the incinerator was probably within 65 kilometers (40 miles) of where the bodies had first been dumped.

Two weeks later, police found an arm bone and a skull. They were identified as belonging to the murderer's wife and child. The remains were found near an industrial site 61 kilometers (38 miles) south

of the original dumping place. There were
three tall smokestacks on the factory.

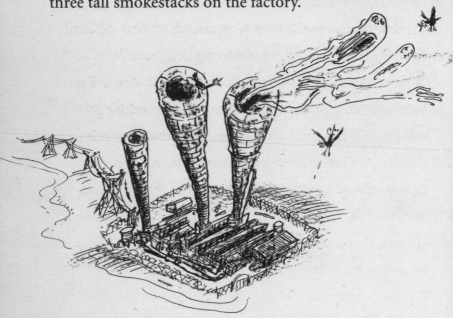

†HE BEAUMON† CHILDREN

Adelaide, Australia, 1966

In January 1966, three children disappeared from the
beach where they'd been playing all morning. Although
a huge search was carried out, they were never
found—dead or alive. Masses of people who believed
they'd seen the children in dreams or psychic visions

contacted the police in charge of the case. But nobody took much notice.

Gerard Croiset, a Dutch psychic detective, offered his help. He directed people to dig at places he'd "seen" the children in visions: sandhills, blocked drainpipes, yards full of sand. When nothing was found he gave out new directions. Local people raised thousands of dollars to dig up the floor of a brand-new warehouse. Still nothing. Thirty years later, after Gerard had died, they dug up the floor again. Still nothing. It seems all his visions were false.

PSYCHOMETRY

Some psychic detectives use "psychometry" to help them track down missing people or murderers. They say they can tell something about a person by holding one of their possessions. Some psychometrists find it hard to touch an object if it has been used in a violent crime.

A GIFT OR A SCAM?

TV shows about psychic detectives have become popular viewing. Some of them are even based on real people. But do psychic detectives really have a gift, or are they just hungry for fame and attention? Often their instructions on where to look for bodies are so vague they could mean anything. The body, they say, will be buried in a shallow grave in a wood. How many murderers have time to dig deep graves? Would you leave a body in the middle of a crowded city street? Predicting the body will be found "near water" is another popular instruction. But do they mean a lake? A stream? The beach? The kitchen sink?

8

SEEING INTO THE FUTURE

What would you do if someone told you the world was going to end in 10 years' time? Would it change the way you live your life? Over the centuries, many people have believed they can see into the future.

Nostradamus was a French doctor and astrologer. In 1555 he published a book of prophecies, written in rhyme, called *Centuries*. His followers believe that many of the events he predicted have indeed come true. They claim his prophecies include the rise of Hitler in Germany, the two world wars, the 1945 bombing of Hiroshima and Nagasaki—even the tragic events that took place in New York on September 11, 2001. Others believe that the prophecies, like the horoscopes you read in magazines, are so vague they could be referring to any number of different things.

MOTHER SHIPTON'S PROPHECIES

According to an ancient Yorkshire legend, Ursula Shipton was born in a cave near a magical well in 1488. At the time she was born there was a great crack of thunder and a wave of sulfurous fumes. The baby was said to be large and misshapen, and many people believed she was the child of the devil. When Ursula was two, her teenage mother gave her away and shut herself up in a convent for the rest of her life.

Ursula seemed to be able to foretell the future from an early age. Although her neighbors feared her magical powers, she only ever used them to help people. As she grew older, the people she had helped began to call her Mother Shipton, although she had no children of her own.

Like Nostradamus, Mother Shipton told her prophecies in verse. She predicted many great historical events, such as the Great Fire of London in 1666, and the defeat of the Spanish Armada in 1588. She even predicted the year she would die—1561.

" ... London's fire will be a biggie ... " What rhymes with 'biggie'?

HINDLEY'S HOAX?

Mother Shipton's verses are still studied today, but did she actually exist or is it all a hoax?

Not many people could read or write in Mother Shipton's time. Her fans believe her prophecies were shared around the fireplace in people's homes and passed on to others. It wasn't until 1641 that they first appeared in a book, 80 years after her death.

Over 200 years later, in 1862, Charles Hindley put together a new book of her predictions, including the verses below. Can you work out what modern events or inventions they might refer to?

Carriages without horses shall go
And accidents fill the world with woe.
Around the world thoughts shall fly
In the twinkling of an eye ...
Under water men shall walk
Shall ride, shall sleep, shall talk.
In the air men shall be seen
In white, in black and in green.
Iron in the water shall float
As easy as a wooden boat.

Sadly for Mother Shipton's fans, it seems these verses weren't written in her lifetime at all. Charles Hindley admitted years ago that he made them up himself. But even if Hindley's book was a fake, what about the prophecies that Mother Shipton's followers have been passing on for almost 400 years?

Death and taxes are the only certainties in life. I predict I will die in 1561. I also predict that I will pay tax in 1521, 1522, 1523, 1524, 1525, 1526, 1527, 1528, 1529, 1530, 1531, 1532, 1533, 1534, 1535...

THE END OF THE WORLD

People have predicted the world would end on the following dates. Lucky for us they've all been wrong . . . so far.

989 Observers of Halley's Comet believed it would collide with Earth.

1881 Mother Shipton

1874, 1878, 1881, 1910, 1914, 1918, 1925, 1975 and 1984 The Jehovah's Witnesses

1999 Japanese scientist Hideo Itakawa used computers to predict that the planets would align in the same positions as told in the Book of Revelation in the Bible.

2003 "Chosen" Earthlings said they had been informed of the date by aliens called Zetas.

And still to come . . .

2012 The ancient Mayans of Central America predicted massive earthquakes and tsunamis.

2014 Pope Leo IX made the prediction in 1514.

3797 Nostradamus

1,000,000 Some current scientists believe that by this year we will have been wiped out by gamma ray bursts from the sun.

PREDICTING YOUR FUTURE

Want to know if you're going to be rich and famous,
pass your history exam, or live to be 100?
Ask one of these people:

Astrologers use the position of the planets,
sun, moon and stars at the time of your birth
to predict events.

Cartomancers use playing cards.

Geomancers scatter pebbles, grains of sand
or seeds on the ground, then "read" the patterns
they make where they fall.

Anthropomancers read the entrails of
human sacrifices.

Oneiromancers interpret what happens
in your dreams.

Chiromancers can tell you what you're like
and what will happen to you by reading the lines
on your hands.

Metascopists read the lines on your forehead.

Phrenologists read the bumps on your skull.

Catopromancers use mirrors to enlighten you.

Tasseomancers tell your future by reading tea leaves.

Coscinomancers use sieves to find missing persons.

Myomancers use rats to locate evil.

Axinomancers use axes to predict an outcome.

Necromancers find out stuff about your future by communicating with spirits of the dead.

*You'll notice that a lot of these words end in –***mancer***. This is because "mancy" comes from the ancient Greek word "manteía" which means divination, or future-telling.*

The mighty ocean liner, *Titanic*, struck an iceberg during its first voyage, from Great Britain to the United States, on April 15, 1912. Although its designer had declared it unsinkable, the ship plunged to the bottom of the icy North Atlantic Ocean. Nearly two-thirds of its passengers and crew drowned.

Several people had dreams or premonitions that the *Titanic* would sink. On the night of the disaster, a 14-year-old girl in England dreamed she was walking in her local park. In the distance she could see a large ship, its decks full of people strolling around.

Then suddenly a loud scream rang out, and the ship began to sink at one end. She woke up terrified, went back to sleep, and had the same dream. Later she found out that her uncle, crew member Leonard Hodgkin, had gone down with the ship.

FICTION STRANGER THAN TRUTH

British novelist W. T. Stead's nightmares began when he was a kid. Every night he had the same dream. He was swimming through icy water, struggling to stay alive. When he grew up,

he included images from these dreams in a novel called *From the Old World to the New*. The book, published 20 years before the *Titanic* disaster, featured a huge liner which struck an iceberg in the Atlantic Ocean and sank. Another ship, the *Majestic*, came to the rescue, but most of the passengers drowned.

Poor Mr. Stead should have paid more attention to his childhood nightmares. In 1912 he accepted an invitation to speak at an international peace conference in the United States. Part of the deal was a first-class ticket on the great ship *Titanic*. He never made it to the conference.

CREEPY COINCIDENCE

Mr. Stead invented the name E.J. Smith for the captain of his fictional ship the *Majestic*. Twenty years later when the *Titanic* sank, the captain who went down with the ship was named E.J. Smith.

9

FIRE-WALKERS AND FORK-BENDERS

Tear up a piece of paper into tiny pieces. Spread them out on a table. Now stare at the pieces. Concentrate *really really* hard. Imagine they are moving around.

Could you make them move? Apparently some people can. These people are called psychokinetic, which means they are able to move things around just by thinking about them.

In the early 1900s, a Polish woman named Stanislawa Tomczyk, or "Little Stasia," amazed everyone with her psychic powers. She could make small objects rise into the air without touching them. Many people laughed her off as a fraud, but she was able to make the objects move even when placed under strict test conditions.

If you believe in psychokinesis —please raise my hand!

MASTER-BENDER

Probably the most famous "mind-mover" is Uri Geller. He claims he can make keys, spoons and forks bend, or make stopped watches start ticking again, just by thinking about them. Nonbelievers claim this is all just a hoax. They say that Geller uses the same kinds of tricks as a magician. While he's drawing his audience in with clever talk, he's actually bending the neck of the spoon against his chair or the side of a table. Or he whips out a spoon he's "prepared" earlier and substitutes it for the original one. The crowd is so busy oohing and aahing they forget to watch what his hands are actually doing.

However, some scientific experiments have indicated that it *is* possible to move microscopically small particles of matter using the power of thought. And in 2001, a psychology professor at the University of Arizona held a spoon-bending party and reported that 60 students got at least some degree of movement happening.

FIRE-WALKING

Could you walk barefoot across a bed of flaming coals four times hotter than boiling water? People on team-building and training courses do it all the time. They're told that pain is all in the mind. If they conquer their fear of pain, they'll fly across the coals without feeling a thing. And then, the theory goes, they'll be able to conquer anything.

Mind power has nothing to do with it. Anyone can walk across a bed of hot coals without burning their tootsies—as long as they keep moving and don't stop to take in the view. It's all to do with temperature and heat. Some materials transfer, or conduct, heat better than others. Think about how the metal handle of a saucepan gets hot to the touch, while a plastic handle remains cool. Metal is a good conductor while plastic is not, and neither is wood. If you had to walk across a pit of red-hot nails the heat would be transferred to your feet instantly and they would burn.

But wood coals are poor conductors so you can touch the hot surface for a second or two without being burned. If you walk across the coals at the right pace they don't have time to transfer their heat. If you're feeling a tad nervous and start sweating at the thought of what you're about to do, all the better. The water in the sweat will provide an extra layer of protection.

WARNING! WARNING!

Although wood coals are poor conductors they are still VERY hot and can give you terrible burns within seconds. So don't go trying this at home.

BRAIN-CHIP MIRACLE

Sometimes people's thoughts *can* really get things moving. Matthew Nagle was totally paralyzed when his spinal cord was shredded in a knife attack in 2001. Now, thanks to a breakthrough in technology, he can play a game of Tetris, check his e-mail or change channels on his TV—simply by thinking about it!

Matthew is the first person to receive a brain implant—known as BrainGate—that transmits his thoughts to a computer cursor. When Matthew thinks about moving his arm, electrodes in the implant pick up the signals from his brain and transmit them to a device attached to his head. The signals then travel down a fiber-optic cable until they reach a cart loaded with computer equipment. Here the signals are translated into a code the computer understands. The power of the mind is pretty amazing.

SKEPTIC OR BELIEVER?

What do you think? Are ghosts real or just people's wild imaginings? Can we really predict the future or "see" where dead bodies are buried? Do aliens exist outside the movies? Our world is full of curious things, many of them "stranger than fiction." Until someone can conclusively prove otherwise, I'm going to keep watching the skies, hoping for a visit of my own. Will you?

MEREDITH COSTAIN was born at the stroke of midnight outside a craggy cave in the middle of a swamp. It is said that lightning fizzed and cracked across a purple sky and the heads of swamp-dwelling frogs and newts twisted wildly at the time of her arrival.

Meredith went on to have an illustrious career as a telepathic psychic at county fairs, correctly predicting the outcome of three National Basketball Association finals. She currently lives in a 150-year-old bluestone house in Melbourne, Australia, which she shares with her partner, children's author Paul Collins, two dogs, a cat, seven chickens and a couple of tame poltergeists named Possum I and Possum II.

You can find out more about Meredith at www.meredithcostain.com

CRAIG SMITH has illustrated over 300 books, including *Billy the Punk* and the *I Hate Fridays* and *Toocool* series. The humor and energy of his warm, exuberant illustrations have delighted children for over twenty-five years.

✝HANKS

Many thanks to all the people who shared their ghost stories and tales of telepathy with me, especially Laila Dickson and Angela Costain. Thanks also to Craig Smith for his inspired and hilarious illustrations, and my editor Susannah Chambers for her diligent fact-checking.

Meredith Costain

The publisher would like to thank the following for photographs used through the book:

Jonathan Davies/istockphoto.com, pages v (alien) and 38
Ireneusz Skorupa/istockphoto.com, pages v (ticket) and 21
Matt Knannlein/istockphoto.com, pages vi and 61
Bartlomiej Wutkowski/istockphoto.com, pages vii and 75
Katherine Garrenson/istockphoto.com, page viii (ghost)
Duncan P. Walker/istockphoto.com, page viii (postcard)
Stefan Klein/istockphoto.com, pages viii (photo frame), 12, 15, 77
Zachary Williams/istockphoto.com, pages viii (notepad), 16, 32, 47, 64
Michael Knight/istockphoto.com, pages viii (UFO) and 32
Fortean Picture Library, page 15
Amanda Rohde/istockphoto.com, page 20
George Cairns/istockphoto.com, page 43 (crop circle background)
Jaimie D. Travis/istockphoto.com, page 64
Sharon Dominick/istockphoto.com, pages 74–75

The photos on pages 30, 40, 76 and 77 are in the public domain.

WHERE TO FIND OUT MORE

Books

Paul Dowswell and Tony Allan, *True Ghost Stories*, Usborne Publishing, 2003

Lynne Kelly, *The Skeptic's Guide to the Paranormal*, Thunder's Mouth Press, 2005

Jenny Randles, *The Complete Book of Aliens & Abductions*, Piatkus, 2000

Paul Roland, *Investigating the Unexplained: Explorations into Ancient Mysteries, The Paranormal and Strange Phenomena*, Berkley Books, 2001

Philippa Wingate, *Alien Abduction? The Scientific Evidence*, E.D.C. Publishing, 1998

Caroline Young, *The Usborne Book of the Haunted World*, E.D.C. Publishing, 1996

Websites

- members.tripod.com/GhostHuntersSociety/faq.htm
- paranormal.about.com
- www.allaboutghosts.com
- www.scifi.com/ufo/
- www.theozfiles.com
- www.unmuseum.org
- www.museumofhoaxes.com
- www.skeptic.com

Watch this!

2001: A Space Odyssey

Close Encounters of the Third Kind

E.T.

Earth: Final Conflict

Farscape

Ghostbusters

Independence Day

Men in Black

Star Trek

Stargate SG-1

The 4400

The X-Files

INDEX